Because Barbara

BARBARA COONEY PAINTS HER WORLD

Story by **SARAH MACKENZIE**

Pictures by **EILEEN RYAN EWEN**

WAXWING BOOKS

When she was a wisp of a girl, Barbara Cooney spent her summers in Maine. Among colorful sprays of wildflowers, sparkling waves of the ocean, and salty sea air, Barbara noticed everything.

At home in New York, she watched her mother paint.
"You try, Barbara," her mother urged. And because
Barbara did whatever she set her mind to, she painted.

But alone in her room, the colorful sprays of wildflowers and sparkling waves of the ocean didn't show up on the page. Not yet. *Oh, to paint like Mama,* thought Barbara.

Each day, Barbara got up and
washed her face and ate breakfast
with her brothers.

She went to school and came home and did her homework.
Pretty soon she was all grown up.

Barbara still loved to paint, so she
decided to become an illustrator.
And because Barbara did whatever
she set her mind to, she began
illustrating books for children.

The publishers, however, wouldn't let her use color.
"It's too expensive to print, Barbara," they told her.
"We don't know if anyone will buy your books yet.
You'll have to prove yourself first."

But my heart and soul are in color! thought Barbara.
Still, she kept making her black-and-white line drawings.
Soon Barbara had children of her own.

Barbara's heart and home grew. She settled with her family in the little town of Pepperell, Massachusetts, where her husband was the town doctor.

One autumn day as Barbara gathered witch hazel in the woods, she passed a little barn. The sun, low in the sky, shone through the doorway, setting a golden stage for a flock of chickens.

White, gold, black, and rust-colored chickens. Speckled
and laced chickens. Chickens with crests on their heads.
With feathered legs and iridescent tails.

I would like to draw those chickens,
thought Barbara.

Later, Barbara found those same chickens in the stories she read of knights and castles. She decided to illustrate them.

And because Barbara did whatever she
set her mind to, every detail in the art
represented what had really grown in the
time of knights and castles.

This time, the beauty Barbara held inside her *did* show up on the page. This time, her publisher agreed to print her art in color.

After the book was published, she was bestowed the highest award for an American illustrator—the Randolph Caldecott Medal.

Back in Pepperell, Barbara set her
drawing table in the center of the
busiest room in the house.

While visiting the family vacation house in Maine, she tucked watercress sandwiches into a wicker hamper and gathered her children for picnics.

She taught them to see what she saw,

to love what she loved,

to take in the delicious wide world.

To truly capture the world's beauty on her page,
she decided she'd need to see the world up close.

And because Barbara did whatever she put her
mind to, she climbed Mount Olympus to see
how things looked from Zeus's point of view.

She slept in Sleeping Beauty's castle.
She spent a week in the Appalachian Mountains
to watch the sun set in the valley.

After her children were all grown up,
Barbara's heart called her back to the salty sea.
She moved to Maine and began to work on
the next book, while a new house was built
around her.

Alongside the pounding of hammers
and the screaming of saws, Barbara
made her best illustrations yet.

She won her second
Caldecott Medal.

Now the very place she loved most became her
palette. From her paintbrush flew gulls,
terns, and cormorants, spruce-covered
islands, heeling sailboats,
and mists of fog.

The colorful sprays of lupines, the sparkling waves of the ocean, and the salty sea air—it all arrived on her page just as it lived in her heart.

Barbara grew old. On a visit to the library in her little town by the sea, she noticed dingy paint, a leaky roof, too-crammed shelves, and cramped spaces. *This is not a proper home for books*, thought Barbara. *No, a library should be a kind of paradise.*

When she closed her eyes, the library transformed in her mind.
Barbara determined that something must be done. And because
Barbara did whatever she set her mind to, she wrote to her illustrator
friends and requested that they send artwork for an auction.

Seventy-five artists contributed their work.
"A howling success!" said Barbara. Her little town
by the edge of the sea would get a new library.

To celebrate, Barbara threw a splendid summer party.
Dark settled, sparklers burned, and the night sky
twinkled with low-lying stars.

Barbara Cooney set out to make the world more beautiful.
And because Barbara did whatever she set her mind to do,
that's what she did.

A Note from the Author

Who was Barbara Cooney? This is something I wondered after enjoying picture books such as *Miss Rumphius* and *Ox-Cart Man.*

Barbara was born in 1917 at the Bossert Hotel in Brooklyn Heights. Her father was a stockbroker, her mother an artist, and she had three brothers (including her twin). But who *really* was Barbara Cooney? She was...

A PLAYFUL MOTHER

Barbara interacted with her four children, Gretel, Barnaby, Talby, and Phoebe, as both mother and playmate. She encouraged her children's creative impulses. They built treehouses and a canoe. They mined for coal in the yard and put on a circus complete with a lion tamer and a high-wire act. Hers was a busy home filled to bursting with children and a number of animals: dogs, cats, birds, mice, turtles, and a golden palomino horse. Each night the whole family sat together for long discussions over a candlelit dinner.

AN ADVENTUROUS WORLD TRAVELER

Barbara traveled extensively over several decades to do research for her books. She went to France, Spain, Greece, North Africa, Mexico, Oceania, and many places in the United States. While she traveled, she took photographs, pressed flowers, and made copious notes and sketches. She always carried a snakebite kit. She loved to come home and recount her wild adventures. One of her favorite stories to tell was of the time when she and her daughter-in-law Susan were nearly chased into the ocean by a crazed donkey in Greece.

AN AVID GARDENER

Wherever Barbara lived, she planted gardens. Vegetables, herbs, flowers—Barbara grew them all, and she especially loved growing many varieties of tomatoes. "By the end of the summer," her son Barnaby recounts, "her big wooden bowl in the middle of the kitchen table was piled high with them, and she regularly rhapsodized over her beautiful, luscious tomatoes. The plants were beautifully staked and tied up off the ground. She pruned them regularly, picked off the bugs and tenderly nurtured their fruits all the way to the kitchen. You should have seen them!" And don't you wish you had?

A MERRYMAKER

Barbara loved a good celebration. Her friend Connie wrote: "Her Christmas tree is a lasting memory for all children who see it, lighted as it is with tiny candles and hung with cookies cut free-hand into the shapes of dragons and bicycle-riding bears and of course characters from her books, frosted in color. Always there is perfection, flair, and detail." Barbara used an artist's palette knife to decorate the cookies with colorful frosting. The tree was put up the day before Christmas, and neighborhood friends came around to look. Each child chose a cookie or two, treasures to eat right from Barbara's magical menagerie.

A GREEDY (AND GENEROUS) READER

Barbara called herself a "greedy reader." Her son Barnaby called her a scholar. When she was preparing to make illustrations for a new book, she read voraciously about the culture and place she was to illustrate. Often, she began learning the language. She had a special fondness for libraries. Before she died, Barbara donated $850,000 to the library, and led a fundraising auction to help rebuild the Skidompha Library in Damariscotta, Maine. She hoped her gift would inspire readers everywhere to give generously to their own libraries.

A PICNICKER OF THE FIRST WATER

Barbara's son called her a picnicker of the first water, which is a way of saying she was rather good at it! "She was way up there in the picnicker hierarchy," he wrote, "producing the finest treats and delicacies, beautiful salads, great cheeses, and fresh home-made loaves of bread. More often than not, there was a serious meal that spilled out from that picnic basket, requiring a charcoal fire to cook steaks, a generous flat place to lay out the feast, and a kid or two to fetch things from the boat or car and to keep the dog out of trouble."

A PROLIFIC ILLUSTRATOR

Over her lifetime, Barbara illustrated 110 books. She was constantly challenging herself to experiment with new mediums and try new things. Though she took a few art classes at Smith College and studied lithography and etching at the Art Students League in New York, she didn't feel that she had come into her own until much later. She believed her greatest work began in the latest years of her life, beginning with *Miss Rumphius*, which she wrote as well as illustrated.

"I'm planning on living to one hundred and I usually do what I set my mind to," Barbara told the *New York Times*. But Barbara didn't quite make it to one hundred. She died at the age of eighty-two after a prolonged illness.

Here's what we know: When Barbara set her mind to do something, she usually did it. And aren't we lucky she did?

Some of Barbara Cooney's Books

1959 Barbara wins a Caldecott Medal for *Chanticleer and the Fox.*

1988 *Island Boy,* Barbara's "hymn to Maine," is published.

1990 *Hattie and the Wild Waves* is published.

1980 Barbara wins a second Caldecott Medal for *Ox-Cart Man*, written by Donald Hall.

1983 *Miss Rumphius* is published and receives the American Book Award.

1999 Barbara's final book is published: *Basket Moon*, written by Mary Lyn Ray.

A Few Books Illustrated by Barbara

Chanticleer and the Fox (1958)

The Story of Holly and Ivy (1958, 1985), written by Rumor Godden

Ox-Cart Man (1979), written by Donald Hall

Emma (1980), written by Wendy Kesselman

Miss Rumphius (1982)

Island Boy (1988)

The Year of the Perfect Christmas Tree (1988), written by Gloria Houston

Hattie and the Wild Waves (1990)

Roxaboxen (1991), written by Alice McLerran

Emily (1992), written by Michael Bedard

Letting Swift River Go (1995), written by Jane Yolen

Eleanor (1996)

Basket Moon (1999), written by Mary Lyn Ray

Selected Bibliography

Cooney, Barbara, and Constance Reed McClellan. "1980: Ox-Cart Man." In *Newbery and Caldecott Medal Books, 1976–1985: With Acceptance Papers, Biographies, and Related Material Chiefly from the Horn Book Magazine*, edited by Lee Kingman, 210–19. Horn Book, 1986.

Cooney, Barbara, and Anna Newton Porter. "1959: Chanticleer and the Fox." In *Newbery and Caldecott Medal Books, 1956–1965: With Acceptance Papers, Biographies, and Related Material Chiefly from the Horn Book Magazine*, edited by Lee Kingman, 198–207. Horn Book, 1974.

Kovacs, Deborah, and James Preller. *Meet the Authors and Illustrators: Sixty Creators of Favorite Children's Books Talk About Their Work.* Vol. 2. Scholastic Professional Books, 1993.

Miller, Judith. "Big Gift for a Small-Town Library." *New York Times*, December 26, 1997; www.nytimes.com/1997/12/26/us/big-gift-for-a-small-town-library.html.

Ortakales, Denise. "Barbara Cooney (1917–2000)." *Women Children's Book Illustrators*; home.metrocast.net/~tortak/illustrators/Cooney.html.

Perl-Rosenthal, Nathan. "What Would Miss Rumphius Do?" *Atlantic*, December 2017; www.theatlantic.com/magazine/archive/2017/12/childrens-books-for-uncertain-times/544104.

Porter, Barnaby and Susan. Interview with the author, October 18, 2019.

Weeks, Linton. "The Children's Author with a Song in Her Art." *Washington Post*, March 15, 2000; www.washingtonpost.com/wp-srv/WPcap/2000-03/15/011r-031500-idx.html?noredirect=on.

For Barnaby and Susan, with love. —S.M.

For one of my earliest art teachers, Nancy Lick,
who encouraged me to believe I could be an artist. —E.R.E.

Waxwing Books titles may be purchased in bulk for educational, business, fundraising, or sales
promotional use. For information, please email Support@WaxwingBooks.com.

Waxwing Books
201 W. North River Drive, Suite 370
Spokane, WA 99201
waxwingbooks.com

Library of Congress Control Number: 2023934639
Juvenile Nonfiction | Biography & Autobiography | Literary
ISBN 978-1-956393-04-0 (hardcover)
ISBN 978-1-956393-05-7 (ebook)

Title lettering by Leah Palmer Preiss.
The text was set in Goudy Old Style and OPTIGoudy.
The illustrations in this book were done in graphite, watercolor, and gouache.
This book was edited by Michael Green and copyedited by Alison Kerr Miller.
Photos on page 42 courtesy of Barnaby Porter
Book design by Cara Llewellyn

Manufactured in China
RRD 10 9 8 7 6 5 4 3 2 1